TABLE OF CONTENTS

To the millions of immigrant steelworkers of the valleys of Western Pennsylvania, the position of reverence was superintendent. Few other positions were held in higher esteem with the exception of priest. The term "boss" was reserved for these middle managers. Growing up among the steelworkers of Pittsburgh, I remember the stories, local legends, and myths. These were stories, however, not of the great capitalist owners (with the exception of Carnegie), but of the middle management "bosses". Stories of plant managers like Bill Jones of Braddock which over ten thousand workers lined the funeral route. These middle managers were men of great respect and awe.

My own family was well represented in the ranks of middle managers including my father. To them, middle management was not a right of passage to the very top, but a profession and a valued career. It was in this environment of heroes, idols, and role models that I started my own quest of the grail of middle management.

My journey started at a time that honored Fredrick Taylor (and middle managers) as the father of scientific management. It was a time that textbooks were written for middle management and case studies focused on lower management, not the CEO. Since only two percent of management arrive at CEO, it is unlikely that CEO case studies have little long-term value.

Industrial barons like Carnegie, Libbey, and Ford realized the real secret of success was in the hands of its middle management. Leadership was the attribute, not of the top but of the middle. And lest we forget, it was a time of great industrial achievement in America.

How did we get from this glory of the 1950s to today's view of middle management? Under cost pressures of the 1970s, middle management moved from a necessity to luxury. It was no longer the Carnegie view of a core corporate asset but one of area cost cutting. The Japanese "flat" organizations became the ideal. The future was in team management. Leadership was reversed for the CEO. Downsizing meant stripping the hierarchy of the middle layer.

This rape of middle management in downsizing rarely saved cost pressured companies. The real issue was the economic pressure of market globalization. Stripping middle management in many cases only accelerated their decline. Without middle management leadership, problem solving lost its focus. More important, the great champions and motivators that were the hallmark of middle management could not be replaced by teams.

By the 1990s it was clear that some of the successful survivors of globalization such as IBM, 3M, and General Motors had traditional structure. Even the anti-cultural high technology companies had seen an evolution of middle managers. Middle management was not the problem, only a casualty of it.

The resurrection of middle management remains slow but necessary. The return of these industrial lions offers new hope in our struggle with globalization. Middle management can supply the leadership and motivation needed to make teams successful. What are needed are a better-prepared middle manager and the rise of the old professional manager model. This book looks at the history and future of middle managers. It focuses on developing professionals with career flexibility. It takes a hard look at flat, Japanese style organizations and team management. It does not toss out that paradigm but integrates it into the middle manager role.

Most important, this book looks at the middle manager as a career professional such as knights and samurai of old. It is for the CEO that must build his middle core as well as the middle manager that must take on career responsibility and includes the front supervisor quest for middle management. The book is strategic in nature, not philosophical. It is for anyone who builds or manages in today's organizations.

PART I
THE LOST GRAIL

"Here lies Arthur, king that was, king that shall be."
                                -from Monte Darthur by Sir Thomas Malor

CHAPTER ONE:
THE AMERICAN DREAM - CAMELOT

"Many brave knights live from a stone of purest mind...the stone is also called the grail."
                                (Parzial – 12th century)

Roots of middle management

Middle managers traditionally have a sense of pride, esteem, and mission. This is a tradition of leadership that has military roots. The centurion of Roman times was a position of leadership. Centurions were respected in society as a whole but more importantly, the success of the legion hinged on this middle management position. The centurion was responsible for a "department" of a hundred men. In particular, the centurion was responsible for training, discipline, and coordination with the legion's mission. Higher officers were dependent on the centurion to implement strategy. The centurion was more than a mere servant was; many times he was part of the development of strategy as well. The centurion was also a great tactician – applying strategy and making battlefield decisions when change was called for. In the heat of battle, many times planned strategy could be ineffective, communications could be broken, and the legion fragmented. In the confusion, the centurion was the hub. The centurion was a professional, dedicated and trained for mission. Never losing sight of the mission, the legion could count on the centurion to adjust and lead when the chain of command was lost.

Many of the great Roman victories were attributed to organization and management hierarchy. The flatter organizations of their opponents lacked strategic flexibility in battle. The Roman hierarchical structure supplied a line of leadership versus a rigid top-driven line of command. We have seen this occur in modern times with the Iraqi top-driven line of command in the Gulf War. The Americans destroyed this line of command communication, and there was no middle leadership. The Iraqi lacked middle leadership to lead. Hierarchical middle-driven organizations are rooted in Western culture and the military tradition. Even the bible uses the analogy of centurion leadership to show the power of God.

Leadership of the middle was the root of Western culture. Anthony of the Desert, a third century monk and Roman ex-legionnaire, based a monastic rule on hierarchical organization. Anthony divided work and management of ten. St. Benedict further refined this for religious orders in the fifth century. In that same century, Gregory the Great applied this hierarchical order to the Christian church. These examples represent today's oldest organizations – a tribute to strength of hierarchical design and the natural longevity of such design. Christian hierarchical organizations and middle management showed the success of the design beyond the military. The same key strengths of leadership, strategic flexibility, and middle management of change apply to any organization.

Early Industrial Examples – the Proti

The arsenal of the Venetian Republic was a massive shipbuilding-manufacturing center of seventeenth and eighteenth century. The arsenal was the world's greatest manufacturing center of the pre-industrial revolution world. The huge complex included shipbuilding, cannon foundry, rope factory, oar factory, lumberyard, dry dock, and miscellaneous equipment. It was the first application of the assembly line producing ships in less than twenty-four hours! While one of the most novel operations of the pre-industrial world, it is the organization that is of our interest.

The arsenal's success was built on a middle-driven hierarchical organization shown in figure 1. Note that the term foreman in the arsenal is equivalent to today's middle manager. The whole organization shows the military roots including the term "admiral" for general plant manager. The very top of this successful organization was a group of well educated but temporary directors (Patroni). The top management was aristocratic and appointed. Their focus was strategic and financial. The "admiral" was the head or chief operating officer of the organization.

Reporting to the admiral was a group of middle managers known as "foremen" or Proti. These foremen were directly responsible for an operation/process such as the cannon foundry or oar manufacture. They managed the heart of the operations. Like the Roman centurion, the Proti translated strategic plans into tactical operations and results. The success of the operation was middle driven by these Proti. They had strict loyalty to the strategic chain of command but were given a great deal of tactical flexibility. The Proti rose from lower management (sub foreman) based on leadership skills. Ultimately, the admiral was chosen from the Proti. The Proti were a class commanding a great deal of social status outside the work place.

Reporting to the Proti were the sub foremen and masters (of a craft). These were front line levels highly focused on supervision. The Proti, while active in supervision, were also part administrator, trainer, and above all, leader. Process and department success was the responsibility of the Proti. The centurion was clearly the evolutionary root of the Proti position. Furthermore, the Proti became the model for the Industrial Revolution's class of middle management.

The Industrial Revolution and Ordnance

The management and organizational writers and designers of the 1800s followed the military tradition, due in part to wars that brought the military into direct management of factories. Prior the Civil War, Cleveland and Pittsburgh had barely three foundries between them – after, the number was over 80! Military officers such as Captain Rodman revolutionized artillery manufacture. The Ordnance Department became the educational and training center for America's new class of middle managers.

Captain Henry Metcalfe, a graduate of West Point and the Ordnance Department, went beyond technology management and focused on the science of administration. In 1885, Captain Metcalfe published a book, *The Cost of Manufacturers and the Administration of Workshops, Public and Private*. While Metcalfe is famous for the development of the "time card" and work orders, he was a pioneer in defining the administrative role of middle management. Furthermore, Metcalfe was one of many military officers to relate middle management level to the rank of captain.

The heart of Metcalfe's approach was to develop the key administrative role of middle management. Metcalfe put the administrative and leadership role above the supervisory role. This was a natural evolutionary step from the Proti but in the down and dirty Industrial Revolution, it was revolutionary as well.

Taylorism

Fredrick Taylor's scientific management was really a manifesto of middle management. Taylor envisioned an expansion of the middle manager's role to planning, control, and cooperation. Fredrick Taylor's model developed in the late 1800s giving more of a material role to the middle manager. More than anything, Taylor saw the middle of the hierarchy as the leadership position. European managers like Henri Fayol and Carl von Clausewitz envisioned the same militaristic hierarchy but saw it as top driven.

Taylorism grew and even in Europe became the predominant approach into the 1950s. Taylorism brought middle management to its zenith. Taylorism helped to establish an academic system to train and educate managers as well. More than anything, Taylorism was part of a growing movement towards a middle management professional. Taylor style managers were hard driving leaders. Like Taylor, they tended to be independent, but loyal to the company. They developed a type of "code" based on the principles of scientific management. Taylor clubs even grew to support this new professionalism.

The Boys of Braddock

The greatest believer in the middle driven organization was steel king – Andrew Carnegie. Andrew Carnegie's first steel mill in Braddock, Pennsylvania (1875) became the productivity jewel of the American Industrialization. Carnegie's secret was to build a core of highly motivated, well-paid middle managers. His industrial empire at Braddock produced some of the most famous middle managers of history – Charles Schwab (later president of US Steel and founder of Bethlehem Steel), Ambrose Monell (later president of International Nickel), Bill Jones (a plant manager), Alva Dinkley and William Dickson (Founders of Midvale Steel), and many others.

Carnegie gave these managers the authority to become great leaders. In addition, he made them part of the profits. These middle managers of Carnegie took a low production, low-quality business and made it the premier steel industry in the world in less than ten years. This was achieved even with a flood of high quality, cheap imported steel and no government support for the industry. His Edgar Thomson Works at Braddock by 1887 held every major world production record. Carnegie, by his own admission, lacked knowledge of steelmaking. He supplied the capital and searched the struggling American industry for the best managers. He then turned the operations over to them, keeping top management out of the operations.

Carnegie's profit-sharing plan for his middle managers made over seventy of them millionaires with the 1901 sale of Carnegie Steel and formation of US Steel. Many of these "Boys of Braddock" went on to revolutionize American industry. While at many companies, these managers formed the Carnegie Veterans Association and continued to meet into the 1930s. These "veterans" saw middle management as "knighthood". They were loyal to their owners but independent and flexible in their management style. They developed a professional code and honed their management skills. While many of them progressed to higher management, their love was middle management. The Veterans Association was a tribute to their earlier years of middle management.

Camelot – Rise of an American Icon

The period of 1870 to 1960 represented the greatest period for middle management. I believe it is no accident that it also represents a golden period of growth for American industry. It was a time that used management to a science. The middle management professional rose in status and income. Middle managers such as steel mill superintendents became the icon of success for millions of American immigrants. Middle management was not a stopover, but a destination.

In my boyhood (1950s/60s) in Braddock, the superintendents' homes were true castles. In the early going, middle managers worked their way up from the ranks in the tradition of the Proti. Eventually education became a requirement; however, the door was never closed to the ranks. In any case, leadership was the major credential needed. In addition, the long line of industrial capitalists such as Carnegie, Ford, and Sloan continued in pushing leadership to the middle.

These "second lieutenants" of industry were American's success engine. In Carnegie's case, the credit and rewards were publicity given. Ford passed on status and money but withheld fame. The status of middle managers highlighted the unique characters of these individuals. Many of these managers became "suburban legends". These legends helped build the mystic of the middle management position. Good leaders at any level are legendary.

Maybe just as significant as the evolution of company legends was culture. These middle management organizational heroes are part of the corporate culture. These stories have survived generations. I worked at one plant where the plant manager was still a legend after twenty years. Some of this is attributed to the Taylor paternal approach to management. Middle managers moved into the culture and ultimately changed it. Successful middle managers understood that they needed to become cultural icons. More importantly, middle managers were real heroes and the only touchable icon of the company, touchable yet removed from day to day contact that is unlikely to produce icons.

The Zenith of American Middle Management

Post-war America would bring middle management to its zenith. The economic boom and growth produced a huge need for middle managers. Taylorism remained the professional code. The growing ranks of middle managers, with small businesses focused a new American middle class. Middle management became part of the American dream. To facilitate this goal achievement of a middle management position, our education system adapted to this need. Industrial engineering, in particular, rose as a training degree for middle management.

The middle management career was farther enhanced by economic growth, outstripping the population supply. While at the zenith of the middle management position, some changes were under way. Education became more of a requirement for career entry. Like knights of old, a noble class emerged.

The Lost Grail

So what was the grail of these great American icons. Probably the single most identifiable attribute was leadership. Leadership was more important than education, skills, and knowledge. This leadership was the middle driven core of organizations. In addition, middle management took the dreams of top management and made them reality. Middle managers were fiercely loyal, but flexible in their methods.

After leadership, middle management was known for its professional code of operations. This was not written code, but one implied by the principles of Taylor. This code rose from a pride in the position and a love for scientific management.

Another attribute of this middle manager of old was a very humanistic and behaviorist approach to management. In many cases, the people they managed were from the social class of their fathers and grandfathers. They knew that people were the root of success.

Organizational Heroes
Captain Bill Jones a – A Young Arthur

Carnegie's staffing of his modern Bessemer mill at Braddock in 1875 was part of a nationwide search. A young superintendent at a Johnstown mill had caught his eye. Bill Jones was known for the loyalty of his men and a natural record breaker. Achieving difficult goals was his passion. Once these goals were met, he was known for taking his men to a baseball game in Pittsburgh. Many times he was known to give a worker money out of his own pocket. He fought hard for higher pay for his men, acting more as a union president. While passed over at Johnstown for promotion because of his "softness" on labor, Carnegie saw the leader. Bill Jones became Braddock's superintendent and in ten years, broke all existing world production records. Carnegie paid him the salary of the "President of the United States". He trained many under him such as Charles Schwab (later US Steel and Bethlehem president). In 1889 he died in a fiery furnace explosion. The Pittsburgh Press estimated over 10,000 lined the streets of his funeral procession. Reporters noted hardened steelworkers in tears. Even into my own generation, workers noted, "I worked with Bill Jones". Bill Jones was indeed one of the greatest middle managers ever.

This grail, however, was not a unilateral bond. It was nurtured by the highest respect of top management. There was a mutual respect and an unwritten assurance of social status and financial security.

Lost Grail of Middle Management

"Take away all our money, our great works, our mines and coke ovens but leave our organization and in four years I shall have re-established myself."
– Andrew Carnegie, 1895

"Take my assets – but leave me my organization and in five years, I'll have it all back." – Alfred Sloan

"Wars may be fought with weapons, but they are won by men."
-General George Patton

"Here lies one who knew how to get around his men who were cleverer than himself." – Andrew Carnegie (epitaph)

"Ever the largest-scale peace maneuvers are only a feeble shadow of the real thing. So that a soldier desirous of acquiring skill in handling troops is forced to theoretical study of Great Captains."
        -Field Marshall Wavell

CHAPTER TWO:
FOR WHOM THE BELL TOLLS - DOWNSIZING, RE-ENGINEERING, ETC.

"At the mid point of my life, I came to the dark wood."
Dante – Divine Comedy

The Problem Emerges

At the end of the golden era of the 1950s, movies such as "Cheaper by the Dozen" were made on middle management. Middle management was at its zenith of popularity. Middle class students flooded industrial engineering curriculums. These middle class icons became career paths for the next generation of baby boomers. Middle management was becoming an extension of a middle class "nobility". Like knights of old, this change took the fire and drive out of the middle management positions. Leadership suffered, and in the vacuum, leadership became a top management responsibility. W. Skinner's book, *The Taming of the Lions*, detailed this lose of leadership in American industry in the 1960s. The centuries-old hierarchical organization became overstaffed in the middle to accommodate the cultural needs of the middle class. The problem started to be seen even in TV sitcoms. Ozzie Nelson, a middle class cultural icon on TV, never had a clearly defined job. This was a

The Lost Grail

reflection of society itself at the time and the overstaffing of middle management.

Economic Crisis

By the late 1960s something different was happening. For years the only significant product imports were Volkswagens and German cameras. Slowly the Japanese auto industry started to increase market share. The energy crisis of the 1970s caused a flood of cheaper, energy efficient Japanese car imports. This, coupled with a targeted inspection strategy, sent not only low priced but high quality cars into the American market. The auto driven American industry was in crisis. It had the wrong products for the market, a history of poor quality, and a high priced product. Problems enough but it also lacked leadership at the top and middle. The crisis expanded rapidly to steel and other industries.

Lacking middle leadership, the strategic leadership shifted to the top of the company. The top management was usually financial managers lacking operating experience. Financial solutions became the strategic survival plan. This led to a new type of downsizing targeted at middle managers to reduce payroll. Many of these financial managers saw the problem as organizational. These organizational "solutions" of downsizing in the middle management ranks hailed the fall of the Round Table.

In 1973 I had just started my management career at Weirton (National Steel). Weirton had a reputation as a family company. You could count on the company for security. In 1973 that changed as the company launched a downsizing effort aimed at middle management. Us younger employees kept our jobs because we "were the future". It was the first time I saw grown men cry. One friend let go was a middle-aged manager with daughters in college. The cuts were a tragedy, but the methodology bordered on cruel. Loyal employees were escorted as they cleaned out their desks and walked to their cars. For the next twenty years, I would see the same thing over and over again. The picture was always in my mind that I was moving through time to this final destiny.

The recessionary downsizing of middle management in the 1970s changed the rules. Middle managers were no longer part of the company but merely a depreciating asset. The middle core that people like Carnegie believed foundation no longer existed. In the companies that took part in the 1970s middle downsizing, organization was changed for the long run. It weakened leadership, chain of command, and made corporate loyalty difficult. In the long run economics were not the issue, but the destruction of an organizational bond of middle management. All of this occurred at a time when the challenges of a global market were about to unfold. In many cases it started a downward spiral of cost cutting. The fact was that the very companies in this spiral were in markets that cost cutting was not a realistic solution. What were needed were technology, process breakthroughs, new ideas, marketing initiatives, and employee motivation. Without middle management to lead, leaving endless cost cutting efforts as the only alternative.

The foreign competition had cheaper labor, government support, and capital. The brutal truth for many companies was there was no financial solution. At a J and L Steel in the 1980s, we were competing against Brazilian steel that was selling below our material costs. If everyone worked for free, we still couldn't compete! Even with a heroic effort of a beaten down middle management that lead the Pittsburgh plant to several world production records – the plant closed after 160 years of operation. This was the story of basic industry throughout the US.

The Japanese Myths

Probably the biggest threat to middle management was economic propaganda. Japanese structures appeared leaner and more efficient. The image of no inspection based on outstanding process control was circulated. LTV Steel's top management "implemented" Statistical Process Control and then proceeded to cut inspection by over 70%. One-week trips to Japan allowed many to "see" what they wanted to see. Whole industrial engineering departments were eliminated based on Japanese recommendations. In my own experience of 15 years working with the Japanese, it was that in many cases we were paying for poor information and some misleading. It was like asking your opponent to help you to beat him! Middle managers who objected to such changes were viewed as "non" team players.

Next came the Japanese team concept. Teams were self-directed, therefore, eliminating the need for middle management. Team leaders from the workers replaced even front line supervision. It had to be good since the Japanese were kicking our butts. Team management became the buzzword of the late '80s and early '90s.

Resist and you were labeled a "non" team player which meet your career was over.

The Japanese Illusion

As the Japanese earned millions in consulting fees from their basic industry competitors, they continued to increase market share. More importantly, they learned the American market. The next wave of attack was to joint venture, which when they usually met, they sold us technology while gaining more market penetration and distribution. The only thing this showed is that our top management was clearly outsmarted. The bigger issue was the changes in organizations infrastructure in basic industry and society. The Japanese didn't really trick us but like our own top management, they did not understand our cultural differences.

Let's look at the concept of team first. On one level, both the Americans and Japanese look at teamwork as a key to success. To both cultures, teamwork means working together to achieve success. That's all good stuff, but when it comes to the concept of team, the view is really different from each side. Japanese teams strive for oneness as a unit. Japanese believe in consensus where team members can feel one with the result or decisions. Japanese de-emphasize individual effort awarding only the team. Japanese would see placing managers on the team as inconsistent. It is this concept of team that was implemented.

American's concept of team is different (even though the result of teamwork is the same). The American concept is based on sports, and this is usually how Americans learn about teams. American teams are individualistic as well. We want teamwork and team spirit, but we pay and reward on individual effort. In our culture we see no inconsistency with this, but to the Japanese, it is an opposing concept. Americans don't need consensus either; culturally we are used to voicing differences, then voting and accepting the outcome (even though we don't agree)/. Americans also are not hung up with having managers on the team (coaches are considered part of the sports team). Of course, in both cases, the goal is teamwork! The problem is that to implement the culturally incorrect team concept causes a breakdown in teamwork.

The secret of team success in America can be middle management. My own experience in winning the first USA Today National Quality award for teams demonstrated this. Our winning team was management driven, not controlled. Leadership is never control, it is always mutual. Out of hundreds of LTV employee teams, our management-driven team not only outperformed all of them, but also stood out in thousands of natural teams modeled after the Japanese. Japanese style teams lack leadership needed in our culture. Furthermore, they constrict the individual that can, if allowed, motivate a team. The success of the team is not in its design, but in its leadership.

Another management problem that evolved from the Japanese revolution was the concept of flat organizations. Like statistical process control and teams, flat organizations appealed to top management because of its compatibility with downsizing. Flat organizations could spell the end of those overpaid middle managers. Teams could manage themselves. It was an attractive concept from body could alone. What was its basis? The Japanese revolution again was offered as proof of its success.

No one took the time to really look at Japanese flat organizations. Buried in a totally different infrastructure was a higher staffed middle management equivalent. The fact is that Japanese tend to over-manage technology and under-manage people. In a non-individualist society such as Japan, this approach is satisfactory. The supervision component of middle management is not needed nor is middle leadership as much. Frankly my focus in this book is what works and doesn't work in Western society.

In our society we have always had a link between social statuses and work at the management level. One of the biggest problems I saw in the implementation of flat organizations was the change in titles. Supervisor and foreman became "team coordinators". Our society did not recognize "team coordinators". I was amazed at how many problems this simple title change caused.

The bottom line for the United States was not in our hierarchical organizations but in economic globalization. Imposing flat organizations was not the real answer. Certainly leaner organizations could help but not tearing apart the infrastructure. Flat organizations lacked leadership and innovation. Teams are great at problem solving but are no substitute for research and development. So many of our problems got worse because of rigid application of Japanese concepts. Unfortunately, our very hope – a highly motivated middle leader – was lost in the process.

Cold Statistics

According to a Conference Board survey in 1995, twenty-eight percent of surveyed companies had no more than four layers of management compared to eight percent in 1990. Only ten percent of respondents had eight or more layers, while in 1990, forty percent of the respondents had such structures. This shows the significant effect of downsizing an organizational infrastructure. Note that the two longest running organizations had seven layers – Arsenale at Venice and the Catholic Church. The Conference Board survey showed that the major reason given (77%) for this downsizing was to cut costs.

An Endicott Report found little or no relationship between downsizing and corporate profitability and productivity. The Endicott Report found that all the downsizing, re-engineering, right-sizing, and mergers went up a scant 1.2% per year, most of which was attributed to technology improvements. Without the massive jumps in technology, productivity and profitability may have actually decreased.

A 1997 American Management Association, while having some mixed signals on downsizing, gave the amazing long conclusion – "In fact, the data shows no correlation between lower operating expenses and higher profits; companies that decrease their costs and companies that increase them are equally likely to report improved profits." This is an amazing blow to conventional corporate wisdom. I don't believe this conclusion would surprise the great industrial leaders of America past, who presented a simpler equation – good managers equal profits.

Michael Owens – a Sir Lancelot

Michael started in the glass industry in West Virginia and Michael started in the glass industry in West Virginia and rose to union president as a young man. Edward Drummond Libbey hired him as a foreman in his New England plant. Libbey ran a very flat organization with his "open door" policy. However, the New England plant was losing lots of money in the 1880s. Owens suggested the problems to Libbey. Libbey offered Owens the superintendent job, which Owens accepted on the condition that Libbey nail shut the door from the factory to Libbey's office. In two years Owens turned the plant around. Owens went on to move Libbey's operations to the Toledo area and helped create a glass empire. Owens always called Libbey "Mr. Libbey" and was fiercely loyal, even when leaving the company later in life. Libbey, for his part, kept a picture of Michael Owens in his office until his death. Libbey was Owens' greatest support and advisor. Owens had some other common middle management attributes such as creativity, innovation, and flamboyant leadership. At the World Columbian Exposition of 1892, Michael Owens and his glass blowers turned the Libbey exhibit into a marketing miracle. Owens got involved in selling carloads of glass as well as exhibit marketing.

Quotes of the Lost Grail

"It's not the position that makes the leader; it's the leader that makes the position.

-Stanley Huffy

"He who thinks he leads, but has no followers, is only taking a walk."   -Leadership Proverb

"The Servant's role is to serve the Prince in the implementation of the idea, to do what he can to ensure the time is right."

-The Servant

"Select thou a man diligent in his business; he shall stand before Kings."   -Proverbs 22:29

"Issuing orders is worth 10 percent. The remaining 90 percent consists of assuring proper and rigorous execution of the order."

-George Patton

"Also worth remembering is that in any man's dark hour, a pat on the back and earnest hand clasp may well work a small miracle."

-General Marshall

"A leader should facilitate problem solving, but let the subordinates solve most problems."

-General Perry Smith

"The union of wise theory with great character will constitute a great captain."

-General Henri De Jamini

CHAPTER THREE:
IN SEARCH OF THE GRAIL

"Why take the style of those heroic times? For nature brings not back the mastodon, nor we those times; and why should any man remodel models?"

                                                                -Tennyson

THE LOST GRAIL OF MIDDLE MANAGEMENT

I.   The principles of leadership haven't changed since God gave them to Moses.
II.   Leaders motivate individuals to achieve organizational success
III.   Organization is the reason for and goal of middle management
IV.   Middle managers make organizations productive – they lead, facilitate, sell, bend, train, and whatever it takes.
V.   Teams don't manage; they are managed for success
VI.   Flat organizations lack direction and purpose (Fayol and Weber had it right – 150 years ago!)
VII.   Hierarchy is Godliness; Bureaucracy is next go Godliness
VIII.   Middle managers overcome people costs by increased profits

End of the Millennium

American industry in the last thirty years was a ship in a storm. Industry did its best but at times, the storm blinded even the best of its leaders. WE must not forget this was the start of a new economic paradigm called globalization. Globalization caused a radical shift in the cost of resources. Governments such as Japan were quick to see the potential, and in the 1990s, the sleeping giant of China awoke. A course of "free" trade, while ideally attractive, meant that resource driven basic industries would have to downsize. This downsizing was an economic adjustment and a necessity. Basic goods would be supplied by cheaper labor in an international market. America even allowed sweatshops to strive at the expense of American jobs. The American government allowed the adjustment to take place in this country. Other countries saw the opportunity and took it. Of course as always, some American industries and businesses even profited by importing cheaper raw materials and products. The fact is that even in this environment, middle management is still the key.

The American steel, glass, and machinery of the 1800s faced all these problems and overcame them. The great American organizations of the Industrial Revolution suffered but adapted. With leadership, technology, and sacrifice, these industries persisted. As today, the government offered little help at best, and in most cases, was detrimental. At time great middle leaders arose, such as Bill Jones and Michael Owens, to pull industry through.

As we have seen, the 80s and early 90s changed the infrastructure of business. A new type of Japanese flat team-managed organizations had been forced on an industry in search of competitive advantage. Middle managers bore the bulk of this combination of downsizing and reorganization required for these flat, "team-managed" structures. The historical power of hierarchical organizations yielded to the lower cost of a flat structure. Team "management" replaced the leadership of middle management. Research centers were replaced with team problem solving. Employee involvement replaced supervising, controlling, and directing. These leaner organizations were the new standard bearers for the new paradigm and economy. Finally in the 1990s, after twenty years of struggle and reorganization, the American economy turned over and ushered a new era of productivity. In stark contrast, the Japanese economic engine slowed. This new American boom was not the result of flat team-structured companies but of technology and innovation. Just as the old lions of industry were considered lost, leadership again was in vogue.

Many organizations were caught in a major dilemma. With markets again growing and technology supplying lower costs and higher productivity, the infrastructure for leadership and management was gone. Flat, team-managed organizations helped in short-term problem solving but lacked focused leadership required for long-term innovation. Furthermore, productivity gains in an upbeat market require the direction and planning roles of middle managers. The promises of the Japanese style management and organizations were not realized. In fact, the failure of the Japanese economy in the 1990s illustrated that their organizational style was not a perpetual success engine. In my own consulting practice, I see a few "team managed" companies still struggling with the eastern team concept. Team management had become the apotheosis of business, yet it failed to produce the results promised. In too many companies, the promise of better, flatter organizations was merely a pretense to downsize or the more politically correct program of "re-engineering". The American boom at the end of the decade left companies searching, looking back again to the great industrial revolution for help. Yes we were in a new post-industrial paradigm but the needs of leadership, planning, motivation, and people skills had not changed. The problem was not the new paradigm but erosion of our basic management skills! The search was on for an answer and the quest was to go back in time. Here was the Holy Grail – old-fashioned management skills. Organizational innovation was a result of these managerial productivity techniques, not flat self-directed companies. Middle management costs, but good management pays for itself. The challenge is to apply the grail in the new global paradigm. The great proverb of modern business philosophers is that we need to stop satisfying the boss and start satisfying the customer. Sounds good, but with the right boss, they are and should be one and the same thing.

Even during the turmoil of the 1980s when team management was the battle cry, many middle managers knew the real secret of successful teams. For some, it was possible to hide behind the team flag and apply good old fashion employee involved improvement. My own experience was to build the first *USA Today National Team Quality* winner at LTV Steel. Yes, it was a team of unquestionable success, but it was driven, coordinated, and sustained by my own middle management leadership. Like most successful teams, this secret was kept from upper management who worshipped the Japanese style consensus teams. I'm still in awe that so many CEOs believed you could organize, motivate, and lead teams by consensus. Consensus did have successes, like purchasing new vending machines for the lunchroom, but few ever achieved real long-term impact driven by middle managers.

Excalibur

In the 1990s something unusual started. There were survivors and new crusaders. IBM – Old Blue – the icon of American hierarchy had survived while the Japanese style adapters such as LTV Steel had failed (twice). General Motors, Ford, Chrysler, Caterpillar, Whirlpool, Sears, and JC Penney had also survived (wounded). A new wave of technology companies had grown to take world leadership. These technology companies naturally started from humble beginnings and grew according to old hierarchical organizations infrastructures.

The lost grail of middle management is really a troika of factors – organization, leadership, and motivation. It is the middle manager that forges an alloy of success out of these three. The three factors cannot be brought together at the top of the house. They must be joined closer to the center. It is here that they are aligned with corporate goals and individual needs. Furthermore, it is at the center that the visions of the top meet the pragmatics of the bottom. It is at this point of turmoil and crisis that the middle manager builds the infrastructure of success.

Old Fashion Leadership

The heart of the grail is old fashion leadership, the type that built Carnegie Steel, Ford, and so many other companies, the type of leadership that led Thomas Carlyle (1795-1881) to coin the term *Captains of Industry*. It hasn't changed from the leadership techniques used by Moses to lead the Hebrews out of Egypt. W. Skinner called our lack of industrial leadership in the 1970s, *The Taming of the Lions* – the title of his book. Of course, today the cry is, we are in a post-industrial paradigm. The fact is that leadership is not paradigm dependent. Leaders are not products of their time and environment; they are products of their intellect and drivel. Technology cannot produce leaders. Leaders, however, can produce technology as we have seen with Steve Jobs at Apple and Bill Gates at Microsoft. They possess different styles but the same high power leadership that fused their own spirit and drive into their company's organizations and products. This type of infusion of spirit is no different from that which Napoleon, Frederick the Great, and Peter the Great left on their countries. Leadership, as we have seen in the earlier chapters, is not limited to the executive suite. Leadership is part of the lost grail of middle management as well as the core of organizations.

Edward Drummond Libbey, founder of Libbey Glass, had only one picture on the wall – that of his middle manager – Michael Owens! Imagine today a portrait of a middle manager in the CEO's office! Libbey was a great financial manager who had that much respect for his operating general. Similarly, the spirit of Andrew Carnegie's steel company was embodied in a dynamic plant manager – Bill Jones. Carnegie paid him his demand – to be paid the equivalent to the salary of the President of the United States (in 1880). Jones, however, died prematurely in a furnace accident. He was so respected that over 10,000 workers lined the streets of Braddock, Pennsylvania to see his coffin pass. Old fashion leadership commands that type of respect. Carnegie Steel was a form for great middle managers, most of who moved on, like Charles Schwab to form Bethlehem Steel (the No. 2 steel company of its day).

Today we look for theories of leadership for guidance but, simply put, leadership is spirit and energy. In my short career as an Air Force officer in the 1970s, I attended an officer's call where pointed questions were asked of several generals involved in the development of the B-1 bomber. One was on the trend of the Ivy League schools in eliminating ROTC on campus. After a few drinks, one of the generals replied passionately that it was no loss to the military that the heart of America's military officer corps was and will be always the American middle class. It is in these mid-western middle class officers that the real American spirit was to lead. The spirit is the main part of the journey to find the grail of middle management. It's like the old story of a diamond hunter who traveled the world in search of diamonds and, after his death, the Hope Diamond was found in his back yard.

Leaders move people; style is secondary to the will, determination, perseverance, and drive. We have been misguided by the productivity gap of the 70s and 80s. As W. Skinner noted, the lion is an excellent icon for middle management leadership. Middle managers must lead bodies while top management can be more of a figurehead (both are leadership)!   Management by "wandering around" is not for middle managers. Lions don't wander the jungle. Lions, like successful leaders, are fully focused on this mission. "Wandering around" works for CEOs, but it's a lack of focus for a middle manager.   What has been lost is the simplistic view of leadership; we have complicated it. What strikes you the most when you look at famous leaders is their lack of training or formal knowledge of leadership theory.   In fact, the grail of enthusiastic, spirit-driven leadership needed by middle management is missing in most college texts.   Business colleges are too directed on training CEOs that requires a different type of leadership. Textbook cases always ask you to analyze from the CEO perspective. At best, less than half of one percent of these students will ever be CEO, and that's twenty years away! Middle managers lead from a position of less authority and a different time horizon.   It requires more skill than training, but education is still key.

In lieu of absolute authority, middle managers depend on organization. A middle manager is a much a part of the organization that he or she must manage. A middle manager needs to motivate the organization to achieve leadership.

A Return to Individual Motivation Vs Team Management

Team effort is good stuff but motivation is always an individual matter. It is the role of the middle manager to develop a team effort, one employee at a time.   In the quest for flat team-managed organizations, the team was the target of motivation. Team motivation is good for communists, socialists, and office bowling teams but offers an organization only marginal success. This is not to knock teams; after all, hierarchical organizations are really concentric teams with leaders. The problem is we came to expect a platoon to learn and execute precision drills without the need of a drill sergeant. Washington, for example, had worked unsuccessfully with his self-directed colonial army.   While these colonials were great individual fighters, they lacked the middle officers to pull them together as a unit or team.   The real turn around came with the addition of the drillmaster and Prussian general who taught them to fight as a team. The real grail of management is that teams are the result of great middle management, not the elimination of it! Why have Western capitalists become convinced that socialistic, flat organizations offer competitive advantage?

Even Communists realized that middle managers were needed to apply socialism. Lenin's first step was to build a strong infrastructure of committees and managers. He was well aware of the weakness of flat socialist governments. Lenin saw the flat socialist approaches as undirected – "Under socialism, all will govern in turn and will soon become accustomed to no one governing". In flat team-managed organizations, employees become accustomed to a lack of leadership. They search for consensus, which can be a slow ideal to achieve. This leads to mediocrity. Politically inert consensus decisions many times lack passion and spirit. The history of human organization is bound in a natural propensity to form hierarchies. In hierarchical organizations, individuals find motivation and direction. Team management takes away self-motivation and drive, which ultimately chokes off innovation.

The American concept of team effort is the sum total of individual efforts. This is different than the eastern concept of team as an entity. Culturally, the West's model for team has always been derived from sports with its blend of individual motivation and team goals. A dichotomy was created as the "team management" approach of Japan and became the model for productivity in the 1980s. With this shift to consensus, team goals, and team motivation, the focus on individual creativity and improvement suffered. The success of the Industrial Revolution was individual creativity, coupled with a strong work ethic. The switch to Japanese teams was perceived as an effort to correct the loss of individual creativity due to assembly type work. The team answer was the right answer but for a different culture. The problem was that we had lost the grail of individual motivation and the resultant drop in "team" productivity reflected the aggregate decline of individual motivation.

Going back to the grail, it is clear that organizational motivation comes one person at time. Motivating people is not rocket science; modern experience is not a breakthrough. What worked for Alexander the Great is still valid today. The fact is that technology has done little for the theory of motivation. Motivation is achieved by satisfying individual needs, wants, and goals to a high degree. During the Industrial Revolution, we sometimes oversimplify that approach to Frederick Taylor's money and inventive plans, stressing the reward over the individual motivation used to achieve it. The techniques of Faylor sometimes cover up his people-driven approach to motivation. As we have seen, the era's greatest motivators such as Bill Jones and Michael Owens were great "people" persons. They demonstrated an individual touch and a real concern for the individual's needs and wants. If we look at the money incentives only as many do in hindsight today, the grail of success is lost. Today we have made profit sharing and incentive plans impersonal. That impersonal approach has left today's workers wanting.

The secret of middle management is to merge corporate goals and individual needs. More importantly, middle managers are the catalysts to make that merger work. It is the middle manager that blends corporate profit motive with worker happiness. In this respect, the manager personalized the corporation and the workplace. The methodology is not the difficulty; it's the compromising that's required. At times, you are on either side of management and workers that requires honesty and integrity. It's a delicate balance, but it's the touch mark of a middle manager. Managing that delicate balance is the very essence of middle management. The delicate balance is enforced by the organizational structure of the middle manager.

Organization – The Alpha and Omega

Organization is the beginning and end for a middle manager. Middle managers owe their very existence to organizational structure. Again, middle managers are the product of the very organization they manage. Also, the ability of the middle manager to achieve organizational goals is dependent on the organization itself. This interdependence on the organization makes the manning of, design of, and planning for the organization the first priority of the middle manager. The middle manager must, by necessity, leave an imprint on the organization. The middle manager has three functions to perform in relationship to organizations – (1) job design, (2) organizational connectivity, and (3) manning.

Job design puts the middle manager into the role of artist. Job design requires breathing life into a corporate vision. The middle manager is at the point where vision and reality as well as mission and structure meet. The middle manager must develop a job where top management's vision meets the lower manager's reality. Without middle management, this welding of vision to reality will never occur. To leave this critical function in flat organizations to lower or upper management is to miss an opportunity to forge the link to maximize productivity. In addition, it is necessary in taller organizations that middle managers have the autonomy to perfect the function of job design.

Job design sounds bureaucratic and it is. Bureaucracy is a lost type of organization, yet is naturally favored by many employees. Over the last ten years, I have tested university business students on their bureaucratic tendencies versus free style organization preferences. Overwhelmingly, these young risk-taking students in a decade of economic boom favor the attributes of stability, clear job definition, and hierarchical career progression. At first, it was surprising to me, but in follow-up decisions, I found the social scars of downsizing in their families, friends, and cultural experiences. Bureaucratic design requires middle management guidance. Too many times the middle manager is asked to implement a job and manage it without being part of the design. The disappearance of the middle manager's role of design is part of the lost grail. The middle manager must function as an integral link in the organizational hierarchy.

The purpose of that link is organizational connectivity. The middle manager takes the idealism and vision of top management and merges it with the realism of front line supervision. Many times top management sets multiple objectives such as 100% on time delivery and zero defects. Both objectives are admirable and idealistic, but on the back shift, the rubber meets the road. For example, a foreman has a shipment ready to go; in fact, it must go to be on time at General Motors. The problem is there is some doubt about the quality. The well-conceived corporate objectives now create an ambiguity at the lower level. A decision must be made and possibly one of the objectives compromised. There exist no directions, only two seemly contrasting objectives. It is at this point of changing entropy and ambiguity that the middle manager interprets the organizational needs and goals in light of individual needs. Without this link, idealism and realism cannot be bridged in the organization. This role of pontiff (*bridge-builder*) is fundamental to the organization.

From my own experience, the role of pontiff is the very essence of organizational connectivity. While this function is usually informal, it flows directly from organizational authority. It is the role of the old industrial "boss" so admired in basic industries and part of the American legend. However, to assure organizational connectivity, manning is critical.

Manning requirements flow from job design and reinforce connectivity. Middle managers need to have complete authority and freedom to man the organizations. Organizations should not be the result of political compromises, downsizing, or centralized personnel decisions. In the last few decades, such organizational manning practices eroded the middle manager's very ability to manage and the organization's ability to achieve goals. Organizations need to reflect the middle manager. Technical qualifications are the least important in manning decisions. Factors such as attitude, people skills, etc. are paramount. In the end, the middle manager must feel the potential employee fits his image. Too many people are hired based on individual accomplishments versus their potential to be a loyal organizational soldier.

With job design, proper manning and organizational connectivity, the middle manager has the keys to organizational success. More importantly, it is a set of keys unique to the middle manager.

Organizational Heroes

Russell Hudson McCarroll
(1890-1948)
McCarroll is one of the unsung heroes of Ford Motor, lost in the countless pages on the lore of Henry Ford. Yet Russell McCarroll was one of "Henry's Lieutenant's", truly reflective of middle management. McCarroll served as chief chemist, research director, and other technical middle management positions for Henry Ford. A graduate chemical engineer fro the University of Michigan, he started at Ford's Highland Park plant in 1915 as a project engineer. McCarroll was known for his enthusiasm and people skills. McCarroll was Ford's engineering wizard, but unlike Ford's friend Tom Edison, McCarroll accomplished his feats through organizational wizardry. McCarroll's teams invented the steel cast crankshaft, soybean oil paints, and artificial leather. They pioneered mass production of aircraft engines and an array of new by-product chemicals. McCarroll was a true obedient soldier, gaining almost no recognition in the popular press or Ford Motor history books. He did, however, have fifty corporate patents that were attributed to him. McCarroll always attributed success to his organization. "In our type of work, we must first have a plan, then a staff, and then an organization." McCarroll also demonstrated the need of a middle manager to cooperate within the corporation. A lot of his success lay in his ability to work with manufacturing on industrial experiments. McCarroll showed that strong middle management enhances even organizational creativity.

FINDING THE GRAIL

"On occasions the servant needs to deceive and mislead – not for pleasure or gain, but to ensure the success of the idea and the prince."

-A. McAlpines – *The Servant*

"The servant must orchestrate the prince's campaigns, for he understands the working of the organization."

-A. McAlpines – *The Servant*

"It is paramount and over-riding responsibility of ever officer to take care of his men before caring for himself."

-General Marshall, US Army

"Businessmen will have to learn to build and manage innovative organizations."

-Peter Drucker

"Deliberation should be joint; decisions single."

-Peter Drucker

"War is too important to be left to the generals."

-Georges Clemenceau

"The people who know best who the job should be done are the ones doing it."

-Dana Corporation Policy Statement

"The leader needs to be in touch with the employees and to communicate with them on a daily basis."

-Donald Peterson – ex-Ford chairman

PART II
APPLICATION OF THE GRAIL

"Who so pulleth out this sword of this stone and anvil is rightly born king of all England."

-Morte Darthur, Book 1

CHAPTER FOUR:
EXCALIBUR – A NEW APOTHEOSIS

"The grail, borne ahead of the procession, was worked with find gold, and there were in the grail, many precious stones, the finest and most costly in the world."

-Chretien do Troyes, 1180

Middle Management as a Catalyst

Without middle management, workers have daily toll, and top management has dreams but the organization lacks fulfillment. The middle manager plays a key role in taking the corporate visions and integrating them into the workers' toll to achieve success. This process of integration requires the catalyst of middle management. This role of integration is the essence of leadership. It is a unique function of interfacing and welding visions to action. It is where the corporation is built and the primary role of middle management.

Marriott is to service as Carnegie to steel and Libbey to glass. Today Bill Marriott is an organizational man and a breeder of highly motivated middle managers. Many times Marriott's young managers are reminiscent of Michael Owens and Bill Jones of an earlier time. Marriott managers are creative and flexible in their approach to make corporate visions reality.

Take the story of one of the Marriott room service captains in Atlanta. The Marriott in Atlanta had always been the host hotel for visiting baseball teams. A cheaper chain hotel built nearby began to offer huge discounts and took that business away. The service captain decided to win it back. On a visit of the Dodgers, he dressed in uniform and went to the competitor's lobby. As Tommy Lasorda entered the rival hotel, the captain welcomed him and said he missed his business. He also noted that the rival hotel closed its room service at 11 PM, but if needed, he'd supply Tommy's favorite late night snack (hamburger and fries). Later that night, the captain returned with the burger and fries from the Marriott kitchen. This personal attention ultimately won the major league business back. The story reminds me of Michael Owens at the 1893 World's Fair going out and selling tickets. It shouldn't be surprising, however; it is a characteristic of employees in great organizations.

Successful middle managers have the type of loyalty that wants the company to succeed. They are natural salesmen for the company. They link their destiny to the company's. This loyalty must be mutual to generate motivational leadership. This fierce loyalty is also a catalyst to motivate employees. As a catalyst, these managers combine loyalty and enthusiasm that stands out. They are natural salesmen for the company. They make things happen internally and externally.

This role of catalyst was one of the first things to disappear in the 1950s, as middle management positions became a type of middle class nobility. Middle managers should be in the middle of the action. It is an interface where the ideas of the top are being transformed into reality. It is a middle management role that not only needs to be reestablished but expanded. The catalyst is that extra role that goes beyond chain of command. It's far more than passing on orders. It's the centurion of old, assuring victory by changing with change. The manager, while more tactical in nature, must always be ready to assure strategic adjustments when needed. This is the missing link in flat organizations.

New Camelot – Mobilis in Mobili

The environment for the middle manager is much different with high technology today. Jules Verne, a hundred years ago, was a great technological visionary, known for his predictions of the telephone, fax machine, submarine, airplane, and much more. His own concern, however, was the future of technology and human relationships. He envisioned that organizations, like mechanical equipment, must follow a design theme known as changing with change (Verne used the Latin – Mobiles in Mobili). This doesn't mean a new set of skills but applying the old skills in new ways or adapting them to new technology.

The biggest impact of technology on the hierarchical organization is a change in the management ratio. Traditionally, 8:16 has been considered the ideal span, probably going back to the Roman design number of ten. For sure, the early Roman design was based on a large supervisory foundation at the bottom of the organization and a large administrative component moving up. Technology has reduced these components at both ends. Thus, technology has increased managerial span. This allows for leaner organizations by changing with technology changes while maintaining a hierarchical infrastructure.

Technology does not reduce infrastructure but it does reduce managerial workload, allowing increased span. Scheduling, project management, clerical and administrative tasks are all significantly reduced. Span can, therefore, be increased to upward of twenty. Considering that technology reduces the overall human resources to operate, substantial reduction is possible even in hierarchical organizations. Technology can even put hierarchical organizations on an equivalent body count level with flat organizations.

Some may argue that information analysis will allow even greater spans as you go up the organization. Certainly this is possible, but technology cannot motivate or act as a productivity catalyst. Clearly taking away Owens' and Jones' administrative and clerical duties would have served time. If you look at their history, Owens and Jones would have turned it into more profits! Technology, therefore, can be expected to increase middle management productivity. It frees middle managers to be more creative.

The straightforward equation of fewer workers, less management is too simplistic. Technology must be managed as well. Maybe more important is Jules Verne's concern of the people/technology interface. Technology must be managed and optimized. More importantly, it must be coordinated with the worker and organization. It is here that a new challenge for middle manager emerges.

Changing with change shouldn't mean eliminating but making it work in a new environment. Ken Chenault, chief operating officer of American Express, is an example of change agents in the middle management group. Ken was a charismatic leader in the merchandise-services division of American Express that sold stereos, jewelry, and personal gear to cardholders by direct mail. The division was a stepchild and a marginal one. When American Express decided to dump the division, Ken put together a counterproposal to save it. He changed product and organization. In two years, the revenues soared from $150 million to $599 million a year.

The real story of Ken Chenault is, however, much deeper. Ken touched both his subordinates and customers. After a 1999 cover story on Ken in Business Week called *The Rise of a Star*, a letter appeared in Business Week's reader report titled, *What Middle Managers can learn from Ken Chenault*. The letter remembered a time in 1988 of having difficulty with American Express with his daughter's credit card. The reader reported failure after failure of getting help from middle managers. "The problem seemed to be unsolvable" until he was put in contact with Ken. The reader remembers him solving it within a week. It's a pure example of what middle managers can do in developing loyalty in customers and subordinates. It is also an example of which middle managers can make things happen. Business Week further had done an "extensive" survey of Ken's current and former colleagues. "Change agent" was the common tag with amazing people skills. The door was always open to subordinates, and his peers view him as non-political. He's hard driving and loyal to the company, division, and workers. At one point, Chenault suggested spinning off the merchandise-services division, and that's typical of the unit/department loyalty that is characteristic of great middle managers.

Middle Management is a Natural

In western history, hierarchical structure is a natural organizational process. We have seen churches, monasteries, governments, armies, and factories all naturally grow into hierarchical organizations over the centuries. In my own consulting of small machining and manufacturing operations, I see many small companies adopt a multilevel approach. This is true also in the small company service business.

Take Bonfe's Auto Service and Body Repair in St. Paul. Bonfe's is a 26-employee shop with a multilevel approach. Management consists of the owner, general managers, and production managers. The production managers oversee the work in process of the three main departments of the repair business – collision, mechanical, and detail services. The general managers handle the mechanical segment and the body shop (collision). The set up is a mirror image of that of the fourteenth century Arsenal of Venice! The functional differences of the units require a middle manager to optimize productivity.

The multilevel approach allows each focus on the specific marketing, training, and unique operating needs such as insurance management in the collision business. More importantly, these middle managers have made Bonfe a leader in the application of technology. The company has six common computer systems. The collision segment has a shop management system and two electronic estimating programs. The repair side has a shop management system, customer database system, and estimating. Computerized alignment, paint mixing, and MIG welding augment this. This technology gives Bonfe a real edge in service. The development of these systems would have been lacking without middle management. The front line production managers didn't have the time or expertise to implement and integrate these systems.

Sensemaking – The Lady of the Lake

Some may say that my use of the lost Holy Grail is an apology for middle management. Old reasons to hold onto a time past. After all, we are in a "new era", a new economic paradigm, and the post industrial revolution. My premise addresses this head on.

Information and technology have increased the need for strong middle management has also increased.

Jules Verne struggled with man and technology in over thirty of his books. In the 1950s, Norbert Wiemer coined the word *cybernetics* to look at management in an automated world. Wiemer was prophetic in many aspects of the post industrial revolution. He foresaw the problem of information overload, entropy systems, and technological abstraction. Wiemer developed these concepts in two famous works – *Human Use of Human Beings* (1950) and *Cybernetics*.

Let's look at information overload. Wiemer put it in scientific terms – "When there is communication without need for communication, merely so that someone may earn the social and intellectual prestige of becoming a priest of communication, the quality and communicative value of the message drops like a plummet". Wiemer, long before the information overload of today, foresaw the issue of communicative value. More information is not better. Anyone trying to research in the Internet understands this. Idealists see the Internet allowing flatter organizations with more direct communication. The problem is that there is nothing to maintain communicative value, let alone improve it. It is here that we see the increasing role of middle management with information and technology.

Wiemer's other insight was that overall operating systems of any type are entropy; that is, they naturally decay. This is the organizational colliery of the second law of thermodynamics. Information also becomes obsolete. The cybernetic component known as feedback is needed to steer the operations. Middle management is the tactical feedback control that adjusts and corrects the operating system. Wiemer noted that in battle, information became obsolete in hours. Like the centurion of old, the middle manager must take over both the strategic and tactical role in the heat of battle. Again technology as we will see, increases the need for middle management.

System entropy and communicative value are part of a larger issue known as technology abstraction or "sensemaking". Sensemaking became a term of interest in the 1970s after Three Mile Island's nuclear accident. The suggestion was that operations and managers were so removed from the operations that they could not fully sense what was going on. The warning signals and computer alerts overwhelmed them. The problem grows today as more operations are controlled and managed via computer screens. The issue is not day-to-day control but decision points, warnings, etc. The process can no longer "make sense" to the decision-maker.

Wiener envisioned Sensemaking as technical abstraction. This abstraction occurs at all levels even at the point of operator/process interference. Younger pilots in high tech jets report a lack of reality, as it appears to be a video game. Sensemaking is a serious challenge to operations management. It's an area that will require more and more of middle management attention.

Another part of sensemaking is to make today's information overload and turn it into a usable resource. Peter Dracker said of middle managers – "they're similar in function to boosters on a telephone cable, which collect, amplify, repackage, and send information". Technology has, in many ways, caused disorder out of increased information. I know many times I would start to research something on the internet, only to be confused and frustrated tow hours later by overload.

Servant/Knight

Analogies in business are too often overdone, and I'll try not to stretch a point. Yet this analogy has been with me throughout my career as a middle manager. Clearly the grail of middle management must always be the servant. The middle manager is a servant of the company and upper management.

The role of a knight also illustrates that of a corporate servant. The role of the night adds the idea of a servant/leader. The knight was the tactical weapon of loyalty's strategic plans. The real reason I have always embraced the knight analogy is the evolution of the knight from codependency to an independent professional. The knight had a code of operations (chivalry), developed his skills, and was a marketable asset. Of course, the analogy of a soldier, in general, works also. It is the same pride of the officer corps of great nations.

The knight's need to be a servant yet an independent professional, however, has stuck with me after the great downsizing moves of the 1970s. A middle manager must be a loyal servant but never a corporate codependent. Carnegie resolved this by making them owners, just like knights of old moved to nobility. It is unfortunate that middle managers are no longer assured security by the owners or top management. I prefer that model, like the Roman centurion, that after his service was assured to become a landowner. The changed environment, however, does not make me optimistic that this part of the grail will ever be found again.

Enlightened self-interest must then be part of the new apotheosis. A free servant requires that the middle manager be responsible for skill improvement as well as retirement. As it was in the evolution of knighthood, I believe this is a positive move towards professionalism.

Team Management

The future role of middle management using the traditional grail reinforces teams and makes them productive. Employee teams are not opposed to having management on the team, in fact; they often actively want it. The function of the teams is to get employee involvement and help in process improvement. Employees want management to pay attention and get involved. The basic behavioral principles of Maslow, Mayo, and Hertzberg have not been negated by the "new economic paradigm".

Even the traditional one-on-one employee/manager involvement of Fredrick Taylor still has a significant role. Taylor's once pioneering ideas have all but been banished from American management textbooks and schools. Once hailed in every text as the Father of Scientific Management, Taylor is now rarely mentioned. This again is the result of Japanese revisionists who pointed to the use of Taylor methods as a major problem in American manufacture. Taylor's classic writings have clearly become a lost grail to a generation of managers.

The fact is Taylor just saw the potential of teams. Some of his incentive programs tired to pull workers into a team. Taylor's teams were well coached and staffed. The Taylor model is far from dead. Successful teams of the future will be middle management led. Middle management insures not only a coach but also a staff of resources for a team.

The Future

Middle management will have its traditional command and control, hierarchical management with its major function as a catalyst for the organization. The grail of middle management will remain leadership, linkage, and interfacing. Technology will force some additional functions. Middle managers will need to make sense out of the technological and human resource systems. They will have to take on the challenge of making teams work to improve productivity and quality.

There will be some major personal challenges to be manager at least in the short run. Loyalty to the company will need to move to an enlightened self-interest. The role of the servant/knight will be a necessary change, but based on earlier principles, the middle manager will define corporate success.

RUTHERFORD B. HAYES
"One of the Good Colonels"
Hayes is one of our least remembered presidents, but he was a great officer of the Civil War. Like most great middle managers that went higher, Hayes' favorite years were in the middle as a colonel. Hayes was not a West Point professional, but a volunteer in a volunteer division, the Ohio 23d. Ari Hoogenboom, Hayes' biographer, put it best – "Hayes understood that in an army of volunteers, colonels like himself were crucial links between democratic, egalitarian, undisciplined enlisted men and West Point-trained professional soldiers". Hayes possessed all the attributes of a great middle leader. He had a strong belief in the mission, leadership skills, and loyalty to his men, and a belief in development of subordinates. One of those subordinates was another future president, William McKinley. Hayes was discharged as a general because of his distinguished service. In Hayes' own words – "I never fought in battle as a general – I was one of the good colonel sin a great army".

QUOTES OF THE LOST GRAIL

"A good colonel makes a good regiment."
                    -Rutherford B. Hayes
"Tactical information which is useful in the combat of small units
will almost certainly be obsolete in an hour or two."
          -Norbert Wiener
"A driving force which as been one of the instruments of our survival
for so many million years is not going to disappear because it clashes
with corporate organization theory."
                    -Antony Jay on Hierarchy
It is not enough to have great qualities; we must also have the
management of them."
          -Francois DeLa Rochefoucould
"The best place to succeed is where you are with what you have."
                    -Charles Schwab

SEVEN HABITS OF SUCCESSFUL MIDDLE MANAGERS

1. Enthusiasm - Enthusiasm is at their heart; they personify it
and create it.
2. Leadership – They lead by example.
3. Flexibility – Middle managers above all else must be flexible;
their survival depends on it.
4. People skills – They can manage in any industry
or operation because their skill is managing people.
5. Loyalty – They are always loyal.
6. Obedience – The only way to have people obey
you is to be obedient.
7. Goal focused – Achieving the goal is their main quest.
8. Sympathetic – They realize that problems of the people
they manage are their problems, too.

CHAPTER FIVE:
LOST VIRTUES

"If many people follow your enthusiastic endeavors, perhaps a new Athens might be created in the land of the Franks, or rather a much better one."
-Letter to Charlemagne, 799 AD

Virtues of the Grail

Virtues are not the basis for textbooks on management. The heart and soul of middle managers, however, are based on core virtues. Education, of course, augments these virtues but the virtues must come first. The good news is that middle management virtues can be developed and improved. The bad news is that these virtues of enthusiasm, organizational loyalty, achievement, initiative, nurturing, and caring have been sidelined. Sometimes as we have seen, these virtues are even hidden in the background of flamboyant personalities; but they are always there with great middle managers. It is the virtue that makes for profit making managers. The virtue is how Carnegie, Ford, Sloan, and so many industrialists based hiring decisions. There is no price high enough to pay for these virtues. Finally, the value is always greater than education and even experience.

Enthusiasm

Enthusiasm is the cardinal virtue for any middle manager. It flows out of a love of managing and dealing with people. William Cohen in his *Wisdom of the Generals* summarized enthusiasm as "a powerful force that can cause an unconquerable spirit to help you accomplish any task or reach any goal". Enthusiasm is the flag of middle management. They must carry this flag during corporate and personal lows. At times it is the toughest thing they have to do. Enthusiasm, however, is the foundation of their leadership.

Whenever a middle manager cannot be enthusiastic for whatever reason, it is time to leave. Enthusiasm is hop in difficult times and the lighthouse for corporate vision. Any hint of despair compromises their leadership. Such enthusiasm requires a basic optimist. Certainly enthusiasm is not a common trait but is necessary and cannot be substituted for.

Organizational Loyalty

Organizational loyalty is the cousin of enthusiasm. Successful middle managers probably don't distinguish between the two. Organizational loyalty is not personal but many times they go together also. Organizational loyalty is a commitment to the corporate vision, mission, and chain of command - in that order. There are times that the order of loyalty is important. For example, many great union middle officers of the Civil war had troubles with the poor generals, but nonetheless were fiercely loyal to the vision and mission. Rutherford Hayes was one of these great middle officers who wrote of this issue.

Organizational loyalty is multidimensional, assuming that people are part of the corporate vision and mission. Middle managers not only lead their management unit but also represent it. Those they manage know middle managers for their loyalty. It is a distinguishing characteristic of all great managers. For people to follow, they expect that type of loyalty from their leaders.

Organizational loyalty is a much-tested virtue today. In the organizations of America's great industrialists, it was a mutual agreement. Today, however, a middle manager must maintain loyalty in the face of an organization that may downsize his or her job. Yet loyalty is needed by the middle manager to effectively lead. Later we will deal with the ideal of enlightened self-interest to help middle managers in today's difficult environment. The old monastic proverb puts it best - "You must know how to obey to be obeyed and how to follow to lead".

Achievement and Innovation

The officers' corps of Carnegie's empire had one thing in common – a passion to achieve goals. Again we see that these virtues are interlocking. Loyalty and enthusiasm form a platform to obtain goals. Remember we are talking about corporate goals here. We as middle managers may or may not have had a part in their development because of this loyalty and enthusiasm came to play. With a strong middle management corps, the biggest problem for executive management may well be not setting high enough goals. Goal setting is a fine art for top management. In fact, the main functions of top management are vision, mission, goals, and building management infrastructure.

Achievement results from a desire to perform; it is, therefore, a virtue as a result. Middle managers can develop the virtue of achievement by goal setting and monitoring. Many times we view as a result of virtue and effort. The "A" student, for example, may not be an achiever. The "B" student, on the other hand, may be an extreme achiever. The problem in evaluating college graduates is to sort out the virtue versus the result. The successful middle manager needs the virtue. Success is the real result of achievement.

Innovation is fundamental to great middle managers. This is why so many of the industrial era middle managers were engineers and scientists. Many like Michael Owens, Bill Jones, and other were great inventors. Unlike the geeks of today, however, they saw innovation as the machine-man system. Former Secretary of Labor Robert Reich hails innovation as the key to survival in the new economy.

Too many times we see innovation as "new" also, but it was basic to the industrial grail. The success of the American Industrial Revolution was not cheap labor and resources but a spirit of innovation.

Initiative

Initiative is not so much lacking today as misunderstood. Many look at initiative as striking out on your own – "the bull by the horns". For the middle manager, initiative is always coordinated with the corporate vision and mission. As we have seen, the strength of the Roman army was the ability of the centurion to take the initiative when the link to command and control what was lost. Initiative, however, is not the exception, but a necessity of hierarchical organization.

The middle manager must not only have the virtue of initiative but must encourage it in all subordinates. Initiative is the flexibility of an organization. We already have seen the failure of Iraq's command and control to have the essential flexibility required. On the other hand it has always been a touchmark of the American military. The Japanese military in World War II also lacked initiative is the officer corps. The German structure, with the exception of Hitler's over control, was a leader in organizational initiative.

General Hugo Baron Von Freytag-Loringhoven (1855-1921), in his famous book, *The Power of Personality in War*. Von Freytag-Loringhoven served in the Russian army and Prussian army as well. He actually made initiative a field service regulation! He stated, "every officer, under all conditions, to exercise initiative to the maximum extent, without fear of consequences. Commanding officers must encourage and require this".

D-Day certainly might have had a different result had Von Freytag-Loringhoven been in command. It is a true blessing that dictators hate initiative and want to have full control. It is this control that is the root of their failure. It is also the reason that flat organizations can lack initiative (command and control at the top).

Nurturing

This may seem like a strange virtue for a middle manager. It was common among the "tough" managers of the Industrial Revolution. As you study the great middle managers, the term "nurturing" fits best. So many times it was a great middle manager that developed future CEOs. The virtue of nurturing is the desire to develop the best in your subordinates. Nurturing involved working with employees to improve them. It is selflessness giving that requires a confident manager. Nurturing by middle management breaks down politics and builds trust in the organization.

Furthermore, the virtue of nurturing leads to job design for productivity. It's about taking unhappy and underemployed employees and making them fit in the organization. Nurturing is part of making the organization user friendly. This is one virtue that improves with age and experience. It is such an important virtue that it is one of the reasons middle management should never be a starting position.

The virtue of nurturing I what puts a high emphasis on training. It, however, goes beyond skills and aims at the individual as well. A broad education should be promoted versus a job skills-only approach.

Caring

General William Cohen concluded in his study of leadership that, "If you want to be a real leader, you must always put the interests of those who report to you ahead of your own personal interests". You'll never find caring in any management textbook. That's unfortunate but true of most middle management virtues. Caring is a virtue that grows as managers learn the importance of people in achieving success. Caring, therefore, broadens the manager's view. Personal problems are part of work.

Developing Virtue

Middle managers are not born. Middle managers evolve through experience, nurturing, and training. There is, however, such as a thing as middle management aptitude. Traits such as optimism, people skills, and things such as socialization are important. This basic middle management aptitude is, I believe, sometimes limited. Negativity and pessimism will prevent the evolution of the needed virtues. I believe what I call middle management aptitude is measurable, although I know of no current test. Not everyone can become a middle manager.

Historically, it is well documented that successful engineers have problems moving into management because of this aptitude.

Traditional wisdom says that there is a trade off between technical skills and people skills as you move up in management. Middle managers need both, but people skills are a necessity and basic.

The real issue is how to develop virtues in middle managers. Step one is to realize that you must screen for basic attitude. Optimism, enthusiasm, achievement orientation, and people skills can be screened in interviews. Middle managers don't start at the middle, so you need to screen all incoming management candidates.

Once the aptitude is there, then education, culture, and example are the keys to developing the virtues of enthusiasm, loyalty, achievement, initiative, nurturing, and caring. The company's leadership, vision, and mission must all reinforce the pursuit of these virtues. Corporate principles must be the standards for evolving middle managers.

Some have noted that many great middle managers never progress to CEO. While many such as Michael Owens, Charles Schwab, and others from the industrial ear made the transition easily. Even these, however, look back on their middle management days as their greatest years. The virtues of middle managers are geared to organizational interfaces such as mission implementation and process innovation. The skill mix of the CEO is somewhat different, and some middle managers' virtues become limited. For middle managers, strength becomes a weakness many times in the CEO position.

PROFILES OF ORGANIZATIONAL HEROES
OLIVER SHELDON (1894-1951)
There is an old management proverb that says a manager should be able to manage in a steel mill or a chocolate factory. Oliver Sheldon spent his career in chocolate manufacture, specifically, at the chocolate factory of Rowntree and Co. Sheldon published his thoughts in 1923 in a book, *The Philosophy of Management*. Sheldon emphasized communal welfare of the worker, corporate spirit of loyalty, employ self-development, and ethics. Sheldon purposed a creed or "code of principles" for middle management. While a follower of Fredrick Taylor's scientific management, he believed behavioral science was on a higher plane. He developed his beliefs in a time of government intervention and foreign competition in the chocolate industry. Sheldon resisted any idea of downsizing, feeling the only hope was in marshaling the human resources in the fight. Because of his belief of communal welfare, he did see a role of government in maintaining global balance.

QUOTES OF THE LOST GRAIL

"Nothing great was ever achieved without enthusiasm."
                              -Ralph Emerson

"The love of life is necessary to the vigorous prosecution of any understanding."   -Samuel Johnson

"I already knew that even in ordinary conditions of the mind, enthusiasm is a potent element with soldiers, but what I saw that day convinced me that if it can be excited from a state of despondency, its power is almost irresistible."
                              -General Sheridan
"Enthusiasm is the bottom of all progress. With it there is accomplishment, without it there are only alibis."

                              -Henry Ford
"Enthusiasm is a virtue rarely to be met with in seasons of cal and unruffled prosperity."   -Thomas Chalmers
"Loyalty cannot be blueprinted. It cannot be produced on an assembly line. In fact it cannot be manufactured at all, for its origins is the human heart."
                              -Maurice Franks

CHAPTER SIX:
A NEW CODE OF CHIVALRY

"Where is the man, who can pull the sword from the stone"?
                    -King Arthur's Legend

We have seen the effect of the new economic and social factors on the middle manager. The old role of stabilizing the hierarchy and organization has evolved into a new role. It is a new career code of cooperation and intrapreneurship. The role takes the middle manager from part of the structure to using the structure for profitability. It is a code that centers on cooperation, intrapreneurship, globalization, and performance. The ultimate fulfillment of the code is profitability. These knights of profit are the grail of the new millennium.

Intrapreneurship

In 1985, Gordon Pinchot defined the intrapreneur as a people with entrepreneurial personalities. Intrapreneurs, like entrepreneurs, are always self-starting and both cannot be primarily motivated by money. Instead they are motivated by visions. To them, money is just a way of keeping score". Intrapreneurs are middle managers that are self-motivated living by a code of performance. The analogy of the knight runs true to the very nature of intrapreneurship. Companies like 3-M and Signode made intrapreneurs, their managerial leaders.

The middle manager intrapreneurs are not free spirits but organizational knights in these companies. They dream visions but use the organization to realize them. Their visions are part of the larger corporate vision. In many ways they adjust organizations to reflect these visions.

A classic example of this new code of chivalry came from a very unlikely company – IBM. It was IBM's middle managers and intrapreneurship that allowed the IBM PC to be developed in less than a year. Divisional IBM managers used an open platform approach, going around other divisions to develop a supply chain for a commercial PC. The traditional structure of IBM is many times overlooked as a middle manager's empire. IBM, sometimes slow and awkward, is a survivor because of its middle management corp. Compare this to the great challenge mounted by Apple with its flat open structure. Apple's weakness was its lack of middle management. Dominated by an inflexible top vision, Apple's strengths became its weakness. Apple's entrepreneurial start allowed for rapid change but with growth, Apple lacked organizational structure for divisional intrapreneurial change. It is with intrapreneur's role to subdivide vision into divisional departmental and individual dreams. Lack of an intrapreneurial culture in Xerox, however, prevented Xerox, the inventor of a windows type operating system and mouse, from realizing any profit from it.

Cooperation

Competition was the code of an earlier age. Today managers look at cooperation. Cooperation covers all dimensions of the middle manager's environment. Cooperation leads to partnerships in departments, divisions, suppliers, unions, customers, and with even competitors. Cooperation needs a linking organism or no interaction can take place. Cooperation plays into the strength of the middle manager's role. Cooperation allows the middle manager to tie together competing organizations for the overall success of those organizations.

Cooperation in organizations takes leadership to oppose the entropic division in organizations. Man is tribal and provincial in nature, always wanting to form smaller groups within the larger organization. Middle managers look to form alliances and partnerships internally and externally to build up organizations. We already discussed somewhat the internal role of middle management. Part of the lost grail of middle management is their external networks.

The buzzword of the last decade was networking. Most of the emphasis was on job networking. What has been long lost is the old external networking of middle managers. In the old basic industries, middle managers have always had a code of cooperation. They formed networks that functioned independent of their own organizations. These networks formed a meaning of cooperation, even within competitive networks.

One of the oldest and still existing of these middle management networks is the Steel Melters Guild. The Guild was made up of meltshop superintendents and assistants throughout the steel industry. The organization meets quarterly and exchanged information in "secret". No minutes or copies of given papers were published. Many times this was to the frustration of upper management! Yet this middle management organization allowed a form for technical problem solving not available in the professional steel societies and associations. Many times the Guild was the source of solutions to costly operating problems.

My own membership in the Guild resulted in many significant but unknown savings to the company. In the 1970s I was assistant meltshop superintendent at Jessop Steel in Washington, Pennsylvania. There were many competing companies within a hundred-mile radius. The 1970s were a time of tight inventory control and cost reduction in the steel industry. At times were ran out of necessary supplies which could have resulted in shutdowns costing thousands of dollars for lack of minor supplies. However, we simply sent a truck to another guild maker shop and got emergency supplies. This was done without paperwork, accounting notes, or top management knowledge. This type of middle management cooperation has been today's model for corporate programs in cooperate advantage.

The Guild also added personal stability to the middle management position by this information exchange. In addition, newsletters distributed position openings. This type of cooperation was a real plus to the parent organizations. In some companies, membership in the Guild was actually promoted because of the problem solving meetings. The Guild was a remnant of the old cooperative networks that can be a model for today.

The application today is not as strong as during the Industrial Revolution, but the potential of cooperation remains the same. Cooperation is the real way to gain advantage. Even biologists are changing their opinion on the concept of "survival of the fittest". Evolution may well be linked to the cooperation amongst groups of animals as well as among species. Cooperative advantage also offers an alternative in the business area as well. The goal is advantage and gain while the method is chosen only by its ability to be successful.

Culturally adapted Globalization

When we think of globalization, we think of an economic movement or corporate strategy, not a middle management code. Yet middle management globalization predates the corporate movement. In the start of the 1900s Fredrick Taylor began a world movement of management techniques. One of the first contributors to Taylor's revolutionary methods was Bill Jones, one of Andrew Carnegie's lieutenants in the 1880s. Bill Jones, as a plant manager of Carnegie's first steel mill, broke very world production and productivity in the industry. Carnegie had promoted international travel of his middle managers to search out success management as well as technology. In turn after Carnegie Steel became the world leader, Bill Jones was a frequent world speaker. Other Carnegie managers such as Julian Kennedy (furnace wizard) took these successful management techniques to India and China.

The man, however, that more than anyone that globalized middle management techniques was Fredrick Taylor. Taylor's efficiency methods and systems approach became in vogue in the United States from 1890 to 1914. World War One made Taylor methods international. The success of American military endeavors and field engineering impressed Europe. That efficiency and search for it led to the ideas of Fredrick Taylor. Taylor never lived to see the international growth of his methods. By the 1930s, Taylorism was the model of American business success. Taylor Associations were common worldwide. Just as a world war brought a beginning to Taylorism, World War II brought an end to it.

It was a war torn Japanese industry that sent out an army of middle managers to search the world for competitive advantage. That army returned and modified Taylorism for their culture. On the surface the Japanese rejected the concept of "Taylorism", focusing on the elements that would not work for them. The Japanese took globalization from imitation to modification to culturally fit. This culturally tailoring management methods and techniques is a unique talent of middle management. Culturally adapting international ideas requires the linking pin position of middle managers. Top managers are not close enough to the people/system interface to make the adaptations to cultures.

The 1980s was an example of this part of the lost code. In the 1980s America sent armies of top management to Japan to look at their success techniques. The result was a flood of unadjusted Japanese methods such as consensus, self-divided teams, open office layout, uniforms, etc. Top management had the authority and power and implement but lacked the ability to make it work. In this decade we see these adjustments finally being made by middle managers after failed implementations.

Performance

The ultimate part of the middle managers code is performance. In the days of the grail, only overachievers could qualify for middle management. Drive was preferable to education. While many of these managers achieved financial success, they were driven by their own performance. They usually outworked their owners.

They were scorekeepers, always aiming at new records. They dreamed of breaking records. Moreover, they set their goals globally. "World" records were their ultimate passion. Bill Jones, Carnegie's colorful plant manager broke every steelmaking record on the books. Jones like Owens at Libbey Glass was a world-class performer by nature. This quest for performance is the distinguishing characteristic of many successful managers such as Bill Gates. For a knight, the battle was the ultimate test of performance.

So what was the secret of their performance – their knights of the grails. A passion to win was certainly a key factor. Scorekeeping, as we have seen, was another part of it. Maybe just as important was the ability to coordinate strategic and tactical goals. That is their ability to break world-class goals into a series of subgoals. This subsectioning of goals is a real art. It must stretch and motivate employees, yet not frustrate them. Real performance is always a progression of small steps.

Middle Manager's Code of Chivalry

A. Make trying new things a way of life.
B. Focus on creativity and new ideas.
C. Reward even failure of new ideas. It's shots on goals – stupid!
D. Cooperate with suppliers, customers, and even competitors.
E. Have a global view but always factor in culture.
F. Develop globally multi-discipline and multi-industry networks.
G. Use network problem solving.
H. Join industry associations.

Quotes of the Lost Grail

"We are born for cooperation, as are the feet, the hands, the eyelids and the upper and lower jaw."
                                                        -Marcus Aurelus
"A friendship founded on business is a good deal better than a business founded on friendship."
                                                        -John Rockefeller
"Nationalism: an infantile disease. It is the measles of mankind."
                                                        -Albert Einstein
"Monopoly is business at end of its journey."
                                                        -Henry D. Lloyd
"The winds and the waves are always on the side of the best navigators."   -Edward Gibbon
"No man is an island, entire of itself; every man is a piece of the continent, a part of the main."
                                                        -John Donne
"Instead of a pyramid . . . the high value enterprise looks like a spider's web."
                                                        -Robert Reich

Carnegie Veterans Association
-A Middle Management Guild-

The brilliance of Andrew Carnegie was his skill in assembling and motivating a corps of middle managers. From 1875 to 1901, Carnegie Steel, driven by over 200 of the best middle managers ever assembled. When Carnegie Steel merged into the United States Steel Corporation, many (well over 50) became millionaires because of Carnegie's middle management stock profit sharing. With their champion Carnegie gone, many of these managers moved on through American industry. These Carnegie Veterans formed new corporations such as International Nickel and Bethlehem Steel. Many of these lesser-known Carnegie Veterans such as William Dickson and Alva Dinkey experimented with and pioneered new motivational techniques. Worker happiness and safety were advanced in new organizations such as the great social experiment of Midvale Steel. Many management techniques spread throughout American industry because of a cooperative management guilds of ex-Carnegie managers known as Carnegie Veterans Association that held meetings and annual conferences until 1938. These meetings allowed middle managers to share ideas from various industries. This guild of industrial knights contributed to major management advances such as safety programs, profit sharing, and gainsharing via cooperative exchanges.

CHAPTER SEVEN:
LOST SKILLS

"I suppose you want your beloved Excalibur back? Come then, take it – and fight your way to freedom".

-Morgan deFoy

More so than virtues, codes, and attributes, middle managers have lost skills. The post Industrial Era has de-emphasized many of the traditional skills along with the de-emphasizing the middle management position. The role model for the last twenty-five years has been toward a low skill position. Skills of grail were originally honed in practice not learned in school. Today a great deal of dependence on education is suggested for skill development. Education is a base not a guarantee of performance or skill level. Education without practical honing is useless. In the later Industrial Revolution, education became an all-encompassing substitute for practical experience. I say that not as a resentful manager of little formal education but one with five college degrees. The skills lost by middle managers are not found in college curriculums. In fact, some of these skills have been actively removed from college courses. These skills include memo writing, inspirational speaking, salesmanship, motivation, ethics, and common sense.

Memo Writing

The counter movement of the 1980s looked at memos as an icon of bottled hierarchies. Popular books told managers not to write memos but to wander around. There was some motivation for this because a great deal of time was wasted in reviewing memos by supervisors. In my own experience in the 70s and 80s some managers were wasting time previewing and reviewing lower level manager memos before they were released. They did this not because they lacked things to do (although in my case this was potentially true), but because they realized the latent power of the memo and wanted control. The real problem with memos is that they have become formalized, structured, and distasteful. Memos of the grail were free expressions and a method of communication. They set goals, clarified missions, inspired, built visions, and networked.

Memos were the permanent records of the organization. They were also the very infrastructure of organizations. Successful organizations need written records such as our governments, constitution, and Supreme Court decisions. Without the written record, entropy, and disorder increases in organizations. Written records, however, build culture and bind organizations.

The Christian Church remains the oldest example of the power memos and letters. St. Paul built, managed, and developed infrastructure over a culturally and geographically diverse area of Euro-Asia. Paul did this while being in chains and in prison via the use of letters. These letters remain the very heart of the church, even two thousand years later.

Bill Gates demonstrated the power of the memo in 1997. Microsoft had fallen behind in the application of Internet browsers, mostly because it was not seen as a corporate goal. Bill Gates, after a weekend of intensive study, wrote a memo on the potential of the Internet. That memo changed a corporate culture and led to Microsoft's control of the web browser market. Memos are community; they can enlighten, inspire, guide, redirect, and explain, as well as market ideas. The communication is and was never in its structure but only in the delivery of the message. Grammar, diction, sentence structure, and form are all good stuff, but it's the ability and only the ability to deliver a message that counts. Too many got lost in the other stuff and that was the basis of a counter movement against memos. Even the necessary training to hone this skill has vanished. Business schools focus on technology versus general education requirements. One of the best gifts I was ever given was from the College of Engineering at the University of Michigan. It was at the time a requirement that engineers take 25 credits of English (more than most liberal arts students). Furthermore these "engineering" English courses were touch, but the English departments best as well as the chair. That education served me well throughout my career.

Inspirational Speaking

Managers are to lead and motivate, if you don't do this when you speak, why speak? Inspirational speaking is also positive whether the delivery is formal or informal. Middle managers further more are always on the job that includes social networks. Inspirational speaking is, therefore, the most used skill of managers. Inspirational speaking must be honest and open.

Maybe the most important element of inspirational speaking is trust. Trust is a requirement for inspirational speaking. To be inspired requires a trust first in the person delivering the message, then a trust in the message. This is what today's managers lack (trust). They see inspirational speaking as in the technique. I once worked for a vice president of LTV who was an outstanding speaker – perfect in delivery. Yet this same man lacked the trust of the employees and rarely inspired them (he did instill fear).

A manager must hone trust. It takes time as well. The hardest thing about trust is that one lapse by a manager can cause long-term damage. Once, however, trust is established, inspirational speaking flows readily. Inspirational speaking is always from the heart and when trust is present, inspiration evolves. Good techniques will always come when speaking from the heart.

"People" skills

Some of the earliest skills defined by management theorists were "people" skills. In the old grail, people skills were a conglomerate of skills that maximized interaction and communication. Today many look at people skills as a tradeoff with technical skills. Managers of the grail, however, had both, many times excelling in both. These managers saw these skills as separate and not in any sense a tradeoff. Middle managers of the grail could talk and educate at the same time. Many of these managers held process patents, copyrights, etc.

People skills were what these managerial knights demonstrated throughout life. Bill Jones, Carnegie's hard driving plant manager, was famous for heading up volunteer help groups for flood and hurricane disasters in the east. While tough task masters, these managers were deeply compassionate to employee problems. Jones was known for taking money out of his own pocket to help workers' families. Again these are skills not found in college curriculum.

Common Sense

These knights of the managerial grail were not slaves to rules and policy. They were loyal officers but guided by common sense. Rules were rigidly applied except where it caused undue burdens on employees. Remember that these knights followed a code of performance above all. Performance had priority over company rules and even policy. This approach was not "anything goes", but a focused common sense approach to maximize performance. Rules and policy were always subservient to organizational success and performance.

Middle managers play the role of "police" or knights of the feudal lord. They have freedom to apply and interpret the rules and policy. They are in the position to decide intent based or global view.

Quotes of the Lost Grail

"One can only do by doing."

-a French proverb

"I'm still learning."

-Michelangelo

"There is nothing training cannot do. Nothing is above its reach. It can turn bad morals to good; it can destroy bad principles and recreate goodness; it can lift men to angelship."

-Mark Twain

"The ability to speak is a short cut to distinction."

-Lowell Thomas

"Words are, of course, the most powerful drug used by mankind."

-Rudyard Kipling

"Yearn to write. Never mind the damn statistics. If you like statistics, become a CPA."   -Jim Murray

"I like the way you always manage to state the obvious with a sense of real discovery."   -Gore Vidal

"Speech is a mirror of the soul; as a man speaks, so he is."

-Publilias Syrus

The Best Horse in the Oil Industry
by Jack McFadyen

Jack McFadyen once told the president of Ohio Oil Company – "I'm the best horse you got". In 1895, Jack McFadyen was promoted from foreman to district foreman of the Findlay Oil district. McFadyen was a driven and inspiring leader. McFadyen was the middle manager that built Marathon Oil (like Jones for USS and Owens for Libbey). A seven-day-a-week man with a temper, he was also known as "Uncle Jack" because of his fairness. A walking encyclopedia on oil drilling, he carried notebooks with him everywhere. He was known as an "industry educator" although unschooled. McFadyen was a great industry networker, often taking a theoretical idea and making it an engineering reality. McFadyen was a skillful master of managing people, but his virtues stood out. Once a bookkeeper showed him a minor error buried in paper where no tax assessor could find it. The bookkeeper noted it could save $800 for the company. McFadyen was clear – "Son, let's declare it; we owe it". It's rare to find such managers today but when you do, they stand out as leaders.

CHAPTER EIGHT:
TODAY'S KNIGHT – A RONIN

"To the right is your journey's end and to the left is your goal hard
won."   -Tales of King Arthur

As we have discussed, the world of the middle manager has
changed. Change, however, is not new to the middle manager. The
old grail of middle management is not obsolete. In fact, the grail
always addressed change.   Industrialization was like today's
globalization, a process of change. The main difference was in the
rate of change, industrialization being slower. The role of the middle
manager was always a grail of adapting. The failure of the 1970s was
that of middle managers to adapt. When middle management was no
longer a source of profitability or competitive advantage – it was no
longer needed. Middle managers lost the grail of knighthood – that is
that their skills and "fighting" are a contract for hire.   Middle
managers have the opportunity to have a major impact. It is that
impact that has value to the company or organization.   It is that
impact that middle managers are paid for. It is why a knight's statute
was related to his success in tournaments.   Success is related to
adaptability, training, education, resources, and focus.

Strategy of the Grail – Ronin

The grail of middle management is one of a contract for services, not a payment for work performed. This is a lost concept in management. Certainly in the last thirty years neither the employer nor middle manager behaved, as such a contractual arrangement existed. It was closer to weak employer/employee relationship. Japanese knights, better known as samurai, followed similar erosion of their contractual grail. Originally samurai were knights for hire, trained at various schools. As time went on, samurai became captive employees of the lords. It was left to a few reformers such as the famous sixteenth century samurai *Miyanoto Musashi* to question this shift. This shift caused erosion in skills, code, and ultimately performance. This analogy is well understood as shown by the popularity of Musashi's writing – *The Book of Five Rings* with American and Japanese businessmen. Musashi focuses on the strength and purity of the samurai vocation and its independence as a service for hire. Musashi's writings created a research interest in career of the way of the samurai. What evolved was a new type of samurai more independent and more performance oriented and representative of the original grail of the samurai.

Ronin Tactics

A Ronin manager must be prepared for a career in a sometimes-hostile environment. Middle managers are often faced with downsizing and reorganizations that change the middle management infrastructure. A Ronin manager must be ready to perform under these adverse conditions. Middle managers need the personal courage to face job "restructuring" (demotions). The Ronin manager needs a plan to facilitate flexibility. The plan must center on education, alternative career skills, financial planning, and specific environmental tactics.

Downsizing

Downsizing can result in job loss, demotion, or loss of employees for the middle manager. None of these options is very appealing. Planning is almost always preferable to damage control. The best plan is to broaden your organizational scope, knowledge, and operating area. Provincial managers are usually the targets of downsizing because they slow the rebirth and healing needed often. The hard facts are the older, higher paid managers are high on the target list also. If this isn't bad enough, the mere threat of downsizing can have a crippling effect on middle managers.

Realizing that downsizing is likely at least once in a middle management career is the first step. Independence and freedom of fear require a strong financial base (we will deal with this in the next chapter). Next is skills and education. The focus here is both internal (applying to present job/career) and external having an alternative career path. A middle manager is a lifetime learner no matter what the age. Ultimately even performance is no guarantee when a company requires the drastic need to downsize. Downsizing is where the life planning pays off.

Mergers

I had the personal experience of going through many downsizing plans, but mergers were by far more painful. First, many times mergers result in downsizing also, especially if you are on the losing side (yes, there is always a losing side). Mergers go even further in that infrastructure is destroyed and politics are paramount. Even the "winning" managers can lose in the long run. What you have is a huge culture clash. In the short term, unless you're a clear-cut winner, plan on getting out. Merged structures tend to evolve randomly over years. There's too much uncertainty to bet your career on it. Mergers should always spark a minimum job hunt effort. Long-run mergers require the same preparation as downsizing. In addition, professional networking in the industry can help uniquely in merger situations, allowing you to be known prior to the merger as well as your achievements. Short term in a merger, your corporate success record can be considered lost. The new organization wants loyalty and cooperation, not previous commitments. Surviving managers will demonstrate both. Letting them know how good you have been will come later.

Demotion

Nothing is more devastating to a middle manager than to be demoted. It cuts at the heart of the old grail between you and the company. A lot of times the company hides the fact (to you only) by calling it reorganization. While side movements are all right in mergers or downsizing, demotions are never all right. Mental damage control is critical in the short run. Forget the company and immediately set new career goals for yourself. Your biggest enemy now is your mind. You must maintain a cool front for yourself and the profession. It's hard, real hard but necessary. No one can defeat you except yourself. Use the energy of anger and depression to dream new dreams, set new goals, and get the bastards back (by honest, fair methods) in a successful job search. Steven Chandler in his book, *100 Ways to Motivate Yourself,* said it best – "Don't just get even – get better". Michael Jordan was cut from his high school and told he wasn't good enough to play. It was a crushing blow, but it was a blow that defined his future success. I often remember the biblical quote – "The sword of victory is forged in defeat". Setbacks are tremendous energy we need to harness for career building.

The greater the defeat, the greater the engine for change and future success. This energy can be used to forge a new career field, start a business, or go back to school. Moving forward also allows you to avoid current advice of looking back and analyzing that results in pain. Save review or "lessons" for the long-term future. Again the best plan is pre-planning.

Ronin Tactics and Strategies

A Ronin manager needs to be flexible and independent. These attributes require financial planning, skill improvement, and alternate career plans. This tritoka of strategies is fundamental to today's Ronin.

Financial Planning

Is the heart of the Ronin knight's plan. A strong backup fund is essential; it must come before all other career plans and investments. The Ronin needs to put investment benefits at the top of the job list. Without that financial rock, middle managers can never be independent enough to manage. Saving is a necessity to the middle manager. It requires discipline and sacrifice, and it must be started immediately. The potential troubles of a middle manager are many as we have seen. Hours, cars, etc. offer no support for the middle manager – only dollar investments can be counted on.

Skills, Training, and Education

Today's middle manager must be a lifetime learner, aggressively pursuing new areas as well as honing old skills. It is a huge mistake of many middle managers to be "too busy" to go to training, seminars, etc. Middle managers should be leaders of technology. Looking at the old grail of management, we see a passion for technology regardless of education level.

Alternate Career Planning

Every manager starting his or her career should immediately start preparation for an alternate career. This is a key part of the foundational triad that gives mental and career independence. It may be a long-term plan to open your own business like many retailing middle managers ultimately do. It may be my own path of moving into business education and consulting. Again, optimizing training opportunities in your present career is key. This alternative career plan must be real working goals, not wishful thinking. In my own quest, I started work on a second master's degree immediately. A few years later I was part-time teaching at night. In addition I was immersed at work in emerging concepts such as statistical process control and statistics. Ultimately in my 40s, I went full time for my Ph.D. while consulting on quality management techniques. It was a blessing and a dream come true, but the journey started over twenty year's prior.

Books of the Grail

Scientific Management, Fredrick Taylor.
100 Ways to Motivate Yourself, Steve Chandler, Career Press, 2001.
Maverick Career Strategies, B. Potter, AMACOM, 1984.
Art of War, Sun-Tzu, many translations available.
Book of Five Rings, Miyanolo Musashi.
Classics in Management, edited by H. Merrill, AMA, 1960.
History of Managing for Quality, J.M. Juran, ASQC Press, 1995.
Wisdom of the Generals, William A. Cohen, 2001, Prentice-Hall.
The History of Management Thought, C.S. George, Jr., 1968, Prentice-Hall.

A MILL LABORER WITH A YALE DEGREE

In 1902 a twenty-eight-year-old man, John Butler Tytus, applies for a mill worker job at ARMCO Steel (Middletown, Ohio). He had a Yale degree and had worked five years at his father's paper plant. His age, physique, and education hardly adapted him to the heavy work of a "spare hand". John worked every job in the rolling mill, but it was his attitude that took him to assistant superintendent in a little over a year. John Tytus blended hands-on experience and paper mill knowledge to innovate new steel rolling processes. John was an omnivorous reader of trade journals. He also followed the written memos of senior sales and marketing managers. He was quick to see an emerging market in lighter gauge steel for automobiles and appliances. Tytus started an experimental rolling mill in Kentucky, the home of ARMCO's "independent" workforce. Working with these "unmanageable" crews, John tried many non-machine combinations. Looked at as crazy by the industry and top management, it would be John who improved steel rolling to meet the demands of the 1920s and on. John Tytus was a classic middle manager, combining hands-on experience, a mastery of information use, people skills, and vision.

CHAPTER NINE: KNIGHTHOOD

"Great care was taken by Charlemagne to provide armor for his nephew (Roland), getting for one who was destined to be a hero."
-The Story of Roland

Today's middle manager faces many challenges but as in the past, it can be a very satisfying career. It must, however, start with an attitude. This is a professional career position. It requires leadership skills beyond those of upper management as well as personal courage. At times you must stand alone with only a vision and goal. This requires a type of independence that must be planned for and built. You must remain a professional in an environment that may treat you as much less. The grail of middle management is a wide scope integrated journey. The cornerstone is independence, flexibility, and resource development. While a middle manager role is to achieve corporate success, his or her invests only in self.

Internal Flexibility

The middle manager's career path must be characterized by flexibility. Middle managers are the merchants of change; they must learn to love it and at times, withstand it. Change is the main difference of today and the grail of old. Change comes faster and is globally sensitive. Change must become a way of life for today's manager. Managers need to learn to embrace and strive from change.

At the heart of a manager's ability to handle change is flexibility. Flexible skills, knowledge, and planning become central. Internal flexibility is a necessity for survival in today'' fast changing corporations. A middle manager needs to integrate internal skills and knowledge. Flexibility to move from department and divisional assignments is the best career insurance. Managers need to be aggressive in searching out cross-learning opportunities; for example, serving on cross-functional committees or taking lateral moves to new departments.

Rings of Internal Flexibility
1. Actively volunteer for cross-functional projects.
2. Learn, visit, and work with internal customers.
3. Maintain a global approach to problem solving.
4. Train on corporate systems and technology.

External Flexibility

External flexibility is achieved through training, education, professional societies, part-time activities, and job searches. There are times that a middle manager needs to initiate change. Job change must be considered as an avenue to build flexibility, not money. This is a different view than traditional wisdom but consistent with the old grail. For example, Carnegie's great corps of middle managers was gathered from stalled careers and career roadblocks.

Training has been noted over and over in different perspectives. There can be no excuse for older managers caught without technology and computer skills. Training is part of a middle manager's career. After planning, training should consume the next largest amount of the manager's time. Managers need to invest their own money when necessary to improve skills and knowledge.

External flexibility requires active networking in your industry and amongst other middle managers. This includes conferences, seminars, and educational meetings. Maybe more important than attendance is involvement in projects and serving as an officer. External flexibility must have priority over internal but really they augment each other and strengthen your career.

Rings of External Flexibility
1. Join an industry association
2. Join a managerial group

3. Become an officer in one of these societies
4. Network by attending conferences

Armor for the Long Term

Middle management (with the exception of promotion into upper management) is a lifelong career. In this I included a <u>planned</u> career change. We discussed the possible pitfalls such as downsizing and demotion, looking at strategies and tactics. Regardless of the pitfall that may include burnout, there is only one type of armor that is general purpose. That armor is spiritual and a holistic view. Spiritual and/or religious principles are extremely valuable to a middle manager in managing as well as living. A middle manager faces too much uncertainty to depend only on himself. I have seen mergers, demotions, and downsizing all lead to suicide, depression, and mental health problems. Those who weather the storms best are those spiritually or religiously grounded.

After the spiritual, a manager needs to develop friendships and hobbies. Balance is critical to release pressure, receive strokes, and find happiness. Hobbies can be work or career related, but they are necessary. Managers also need vacations, not only to relax but to recharge. Bill Gates' two-week reading holidays have not only recharged him, but Microsoft. I used one day reading vacations to do the same. I personally found mind stretching vacations such as Williamsburg, Washington, DC, etc. to be enjoyable to the family while being a catalyst of creative ideas. Sitting on the beach did little for me. But however or wherever you do vacation – do it. For example, today I love one-day trips to Ann Arbor to refresh and recharge. Some people (I'm not one of them) have mastered the one-hour vacation as well.

Another area of importance is that of health (mental and physical). Vitamins and exercise are important. Middle managers are also extremely addictive to negative energy outlets such as smoking, drinking, and under/over eating. Sometimes these things are used to help sustain power drives. This is an area that must be researched and developed for each individual manager.

As we have discussed, financial planning and aggressive saving is the best armor. If it's your first job, set aside a large percent and hold to it, only increasing. If you are later in your career, start putting away a large percentage of your raises. Aggressive saving and investment is part of your middle management career management.

After money, skills and education are part of the needed armor. This is a lifetime strategy. You must improve and <u>add</u> new skills throughout your career. Tied with that effort is the development of an alternative career. The prime years for a middle manager are 30 to 45. At 45 you should be prepared, if necessary, to start an alternate career. Alternate career planning starts day one of the first job. That plan will require coordination of resources. At age 45 to 50, that plan must be in the ready mode.

Forging of Armor

1. Select and start your alternative career plan right now.
2. Start an aggressive saving plan right now.
3. Search out cross-functional committees, projects, etc. to get involved in.
4. Select new skills to learn.
5. Go back to school for another or advanced degree.
6. Become active in a professional society.
7. Serve on an industry committee.

Camelot – Retirement

Knighthood, like middle management, is a lifelong career. Retirement is only the last phase of the career journey. Retirement must be viewed in holistic terms, not as freedom from job chains. Middle managers must plan for the last phase of the career, whether that is an alternate career or some natural extension such as writing, teaching, or consulting. The whole career should be a gathering and developing of resources.

The very nature of a life of training and skills development leads to a different type of retirement. Middle managers should retire into volunteer work, education, and other constructive venues, remembering that middle management is a brotherhood of managers.

INDEX